COLONNA FELICE

TRANSPARENCY

EDITIONS MATERANE

INDEX

“ Quantum mutata ab illa!”

Quantum mutata ab illa!
You see, dear,
the rosy dawn prodromes
already tinged
the eastern sky.
You doze
and complaints
if only infinity
your pretty face
or the white your arm.
"Quantum changed ab illa! "-
finds my mind enamored
like once.
On impulse I wonder
If occupations and daily penis
for not easy
family and friendship relations
does not have gradually turned off in you

the ardor of passion
and every effort of love.

As the years they gallop,
I leaden promises life
which is to come.
Liberate yourself from your phobias
And serene goes towards to life
Fleeing.
It can be still clear
Your heaven,
If you only want it
And you abandon yourself to the pleasures of love
And to indulgence towards the inevitable
Adversities of life.
And 'sweet think of you,
But it's hard not to have you near
With the mind and heart.
You digress
Towards trembling horizons
It will close in silence.

Good night, my soul.
Already asleep,
but continues to be
In my thoughts
and then some in my dreams.
Sweet dreams, my love.
While, half-asleep,
I try and infinity your arm
and intertwining my fingers
to your already submissive,
listen to your rhythmic breathing.
I sigh and look after you wake
from the first deep sleep
and already a foretaste of the sweetness
the longed embrace,
while the accomplice Diana,
sister of Phoebus Apollo dormant,
It shines fully in heaven.
"Trust me love talks"
It brings us the slow
Morning awakening
He poured the peace of the evening.

Your boss
On my chest,
Your arm bound
Such as lace,
I say words of honey,
And you strengthen your grip
And as a cat meow
In heat.
But sometimes for a trifle
I Serb resentment
And I incline only their backs,
very similar to the Moon crowds.

Only I ask
You leave me
dream again
Clear skies,
Blue sea
And snow-covered mountains.
And you just ask me
Quiet life
And transparency of thoughts,
I love sincere and unique.
It is too precious
Marital happiness.
You know, I know.
But we do not cost anything
protect her,
Because the half-century love
And 'diamond stone.

11

Thank you, Sir,
for giving me
this companion
and not the other.
Beautiful, honest,
intelligent, human.
Perfect wife,
caring and wise mother,
where you have printed
the purest imprint
of Your Love.
Please, Lord,
guard it always
for his sake, my
and our children and grandchildren.
Secure to her happiness family and marriage
and physical well-being
for all earthly life.
Reserve her and all of us
the unearthly happiness
in Your heavenly Kingdom.

In private

Others may not want
Who is in love like me.
being alone
It is congenial to love nature.
Sometimes just
Watching you shut up and think.
And a few words
enough
To break the silence talkative.
My caresses,
Your blush
just as well
To sing a song of love
And touch the sky with a finger.

Contract of love
-"Love"
Do you want me to call you so?
I do not naturally
Since you have wounded
My heart.
My pride cries ...
But my heart
Still beats when
You comes near me
to hug me.
If you really do not want
I banish you for ever,
Solemn promise you make me.
Show me your
True love always.
Because your are not
Words to the wind
Scattered into the void,
You must prove them
With concrete action
And transparent sincerity.

.

Others do not ask

What to test.

I would never lose you forever!

Belvedere on "Sassi"

Can not fail us, dear,
The climb to Belvedere.
What a spectacle presents
Our astonished eyes!
Faced,
On the hilly ridge
The huge dragon
New Matera
Stretched for several kilometers
From North to south.
Down in the deep ravine
The namesake river
It takes place tortuous and sleepy.
Blowing mild and steady wind
It messes up gently
Your silky long hair
While I fixed on the other bank steep
The access cavity

The ancient stone churches.
Then ask me to venture
Among those below the Belvedere
And you go into raptures
To contemplate and study
The shreds of paintings
Of saints and sacred history.
Finally lead me almost reluctant
Among the stones murgian
To explore the plateau.
And look for some secluded place
To cover me with kisses
And hold me to your chest,
Drunk with happiness
For an unusual day.

INTERVIEW

Because now it is more urgent
Your invitation to make You visit
In Your Temple?
As a teenager I had the opportunity
More closely know You
And beg You with the heart
And not just lip service.
Then earthly love for the woman,
With multiple faces, and finally
With one beautiful face,
Gradually she distracted me from You.
And I walked away from Your Home,
While aware of Thy omnipresence.
With the companion of life that you gave me
(Alas, feebly!)
I did know from my children.
As part of a Pastoral Group
And even more through theological readings
I realized that You are really

The Lord of the universe and of history,
the Alpha and the Omega of all creation
and of every human life.
With reason!
But his heart was still warm, the mind
Easy to distraction to the joys and sorrows
Of everyday life and work.
Therefore I beg
Always welcome me, despite my weaknesses and shortcomings.
And I beg you to turn even more
My heart and to strengthen my will
To adjust my conduct life
Thy eternal Word of love
Father, Son and Holy Spirit.

In the "Sassi of Matera" at sunset
Until the fifties

Or that in the neighborhood court
Sirius slowly hide oneself
Behind the Apennines,
It dampens the noise of children.
One by one come out of the cave dwellings
The mothers and daughters of marriageable
That have already prepared
The modest dinner to their husbands or fathers.
Han time till dusk and beyond,
To gossip or complain,
When tired and hungry
The men return from the fields sown
Or from small vegetable gardens or by its own vineyard
sometimes the property of others.
The donkey or mule to them before
Advancing clogs on the uneven pavement.

What more swollen what less
Swing saddlebags
And he sings the source of water in the barrels.
The flasks are empty, more than that of water wine.
The frugal meal restores them, wine, precious
And, therefore, mixed with water, it quenches them.
Then seated on the low wall decorated
Aspire tobacco pipe from elderly
O with a fresh joint of the patient invoice.
Han little time to exchange
A few words with the neighbors,
Already that fatigue of the hard work
Now it takes over and fall
The eyelids, from time to time.
Housewives have cleared
It washed the dishes, not many.
Now put to bed their men and children,
Turn off the lights and expensive return

To confabulate with nearby.
What ever they say to each other?
It 'easy to say: births, marriages and deaths,
Sons and pains, joys and sorrows,
Hopes and disappointments.
Even the trend of the time
It is a recurring theme, because of the whims of the sky
It depends on every ear, every legume,
Each vine trunk, each orchard gift,
Wild every grass or medicine.
Simple and hard life, marked
By incessant each of the seasons.
Short life due to all kinds of evil,
Which does not spare children, pregnant women,
Nursing bitches, men exhausted by fatigue
From the first morning to late evening,
More rarely by older wrinkled skin.
Yet quiet life, rather than in the postwar period
Busy, pressed by the alleged progress.

And you welcome
Pleased with me
His usual colors:
Yellow, reddish brown.
leaves fall
One by one
By the breath of the breeze.
And my spirit
Rests in you
How about soft blanket
That the dark earth,
No more green,
welcomes in accumulation.
…Everything's quiet,
... Everything is peace!

Choke me with kisses,
Fill me with caresses,
Promise eternal love,
Even if I do not deserve it
At all
For my misunderstanding
And my innate sexism.
Do I always live next door,
Next to you,
Only woman and mistress
Of my life.
Come on, smile back
As always you did
In so many beautiful moments,
Always live in the memory,
forever indelible.

VALENTINE'S DAY

By the ban,
Today,
To all kinds of anguish and concern.
Clear your mind
On every shadow that oppresses.
It is just light
In your soul
And renewed passion
In your heart.
And 'a special day
Ranging celebrated
In a unique way,
Between the two of us only,
Absolute intimacy.
It 's the gift I ask.
And you ask
any gift
Can make you completely happy

And stare into memory
The only joy
Of such day
Of married life.
Saying "I love you" is probably very little.
The truth is that I love you like a goddess.
And so I hope to be able to live
Much longer by your side,
Protected by the Holy presiding Love.

Put aside not for us,
Shining stars,
the extreme misfortune
who fears
every loving heart.
She split from me ...
Oh, I never stand it!
Dark thoughts,
insane projects
Perhaps she feeds
From that time poor
where she staggered
his faith in me.
I would give my life
to revive
and heart put them in peace,
then she is
my only beloved,
my only hope.

If it's true
That even accept me
What lover and groom
Indissolubly united to you,
It 'also true
That your confidence wobbles
It gnaws the latent jealousy
Believe me – unmotivaded.
What evidence yet
Do you wait?
We love you still
As always
And I could never…
Do without you!

From the stars I would crash
Into the abyss,
If you love me stop
For your or my fault.
The sky of my soul
It would always be covered with envy
Or exactly like the night.
Darkness would be the future,
Off all hope of life.

Such you seamed to me that day,
which I know you now and I love you.
Not even the voracious Time
He has mercilessly ribbed
Your bright face
Or the velvety cheeks.
Neither ruffled your pink lips
Or your alabaster neck.
Nor pendulous is already
Your fragrant breasts
Or streaked with purple veins
Your smooth legs.
Six as is
It never grows old ...
I still hope for a long ...

Ceases to picture
Which villain spouse
Man who has violated unjustly
The wedding ring.
It 's true: I have lost the wedding ring,
But for stupid fatality!
It's never changed
The feeling I have for you
In the depths of the heart.
And my thought
Is always
Looking to you only.
Believe me:
It is the only reality!

Whatever it was
Your homeland,
The condition of your ancestors
And your parents,
At your first appearance
Fresh sixteen year old, beautiful,
Bright and jolly,
I would have been bound
In perennials chains.
If you'd seen
In threadbare clothing
Cinderella.
If I had had
A link with another
Or you were already committed.
All I would do
To breach
In your heart
And to make you fall in love with me.
Everything, to take you to the altar!

Keep in your hands
The key
The great mystery
Love.
Keep in your hands
My past life, present and future. To you turns my every thought,
All my anxiety,
All my fears.
Eternal love
To you tie me.
From you flows
My every hope
Of human salvation
And after death,
From you, God-fearing,
From you, absolute moral value.

How the Sun again
every morning,
It is new every day
the emotion that gives me
Your slow awakening.
Sometimes laughing your face,
when your sky,
our sky,
He is cloudless.
Other times your eyes
show fixity,
When a worry gnaws
and you are insensitive to my every caress.
With difficulty then you untie
and invite me to patience.
What I ask
it's just that you do it
Gently ...
always!

Your delicate limbs
all
Inspire me love:
But it is not only flame
The fire in my heart,
When, even more than a monarch,
I love your beautiful eyes,
The roses of your mouth, Your
pearly breast,
Your pelvis as a dancer,
Your tapered legs,
Your soft, warm hands,
Your feet fairy.
Oh, do not subtract
To my view,
The warmth of my kisses,
Passion without brake
Of my senses!

I could not tolerate
That your beautiful eyelashes
they were wet
Even a single tear.
Gaze at in the entire light
And never insult you
It is my only the Desire.
I would never be ungrateful
To your sincere love.
I disarms even
Your gaze
And therefore I could never really betray you.
Trust and put to flight
Your every fear.
My future is only
In your hands :
Never foul I committed,
However it would be mild foul.

Come, follow my steps,
truncates any delay.
Beyond the horizon,
There awaits a life
still happy,
in spite of all the bitterness
that everyday life
There pantry,
sometimes with both hands.
Together
everything we still face
holding hands
and heat us each other.

Most sweet laces
Of Love and Hymen
There wraped up us forever
The day the dog days in 1947.
From that joy of Heaven
Only warm embraces
And tender kisses
I expected from you,
dear wife and lover,
My hope,
sweet splendor of my watch.
Oh, never steal
The perfect marital bliss,
It is in good
That in bad destiny
While an indissoluble love
It binds us!

I burn as a time
The gleam of your beautiful eyes.
Shut up if you want me to say
That still haunt you
Sad thoughts and dull resentment
Old now.
You have no reason,
If for months
-So seemed-
You gave evidence of having passed
Any resurgence of intolerance
And the instinctive hatred,
Thanks to the love you always.
I am here, next to you,
Get enough of your sight,
And I expect you to tell me that,
In addition to the new hat,
Are you ready to give me
A happy Christmas
Like countless others,
The warmth of the family.

As a swarm of bees
Flying playful and tender Cupids
Towards my angelic Rosa,
Gentle as the namesake flower.
It matters little green men ages:
Li attracts your beautiful face,
Never changed, Madonna,
The twinkling of your eyes
When you laugh, carefree,
The smell of your skin velvety
When the smell,
The sweet music of your words
When tenderness invades
Your heart.
They are welcome,
Because bring me
Peace in the heart
And the end of Sighs
Apprehension.

Ode to Matera City (Heritage of the Unesco) - Candidate for European Capital of Culture 2019

ODE TO MATERA

Here is a day
I am beset by the desire
Getting lonely
On the Belvedere,
Dominating the Gravina
And light, in front,
The sinuous serpent of Matera.
I seem to hear
Not already the clear waters rustling,
But the lament of the stream
For the foam that the drowning,
For wastes linger
Its flow singing.
I go down over the balustrade
And I walk the difficult path

Which leads down
Towards the front covers caves,
Watching the city
How sleepy eyes
And they tell ...
They tell of very ancient times,
Of ancestors coexisted with stone
And when the stone is provided to themselves
To cease the bad weather,
In small groups, they got,
For the stunted survival,
Now known healthy herbs
Or fresh meat and game,
Almost always insufficient
For many mouths to feed.
Tell of humble villages entrenched,
Of exhausting toil
To get food,
Storing rainwater,
Defend themselves from wild beasts
Or from threatening nomads.

Centuries pass
And civilization walking here:
It is learned and passed
The workings of the stone tool
And sharp weapons,
Or the workings of the bones for everyday users.
Then known as copper, bronze, iron,
And raids, the cruelty of the winners warriors
In their pitches planted with fatigue
Or in coarse fences of small livestock.
For centuries and centuries are at best semi-free
And always serve new masters:
Preitalici, Achaean, Greeks, Romans,
Then barbarians, Saracens, Byzantines,
Normans, Swabians, Angevins and Aragonese,
French and Spanish. And fans of
The Kingdom of the Two Sicilies,
They are property of the Bourbons.
But the Murgia is remote from the din Of armies,
it is home to the holy hermits

O monasteries praying, that they dig into the rock

Chapels and small sanctuaries.
Oh! Medieval mystic and reciting the litany,
Steeped in popular piety and pious pilgrimages
The high houses of the Christian God and the Holy Mother.
But alas! Afterwards, in the following centuries,
The ruins of Time and the weakening of the Faith
They reduced to fences many churches jewels
Rock, painted by art patient
Of Oriental and Byzantine monks ..
And the frantic search for a few returned
Recently, many relics of the ancient fathers,
And still many Superintendences will return
Humanity today and tomorrow.
You, lonely passenger,
And you, a tourist group,

Paused in meditation
Before every witness
Antique feel, suffer and build,
With the veneration of an heir
That everything has to the past!

Inauspicious year
of the distance
For reasons fools

And perhaps only out of pride!
How many cold, dark evenings
The tedious and long winter
I walked,
Lonely lover,
Not knowing
where go
And dying of nostalgia:
There were even the stars
Confide my pain.
But seasonal
Companions, at least, I had
Stray little fire-flies,
Beautiful of flashing lights,
Which I delivered my frequent
Sighs of hope ...
To hear from and see you again at last

To say that nothing had changed
And my heart
It was still all yours.

Already the Aurora
He abandons the thalamus Titone,

the dawn is already vermilion
vanishes and black mantle
of the night.
I see in you
purple pink
And I kiss your beautiful hand,
Holding the thread of my life.
Silent our tongues
And you do chain of my arms.
I will seal with my biting his lips.
Joust in jest
Our love languages.
And I pray the Destiny
You'll never divide
From my eyes
Always enchanted.

Dolce is knowing
On being loved, loving.

But to me martyrdom to the heart
Your changing humor,
The long silences,
Deaf grudges
Against misunderstood,
suspects
And fervent fantasies
For whom nothing is real.
Even more than now
I do not lose occasions
to show
The my undchanged And unchanging love.

When you're gone,
I think an hour long

One thousand years
And my thought Followers
As the shadow the object
That sunlight passes through.
Where are you?
Whom are you with?
A hard drive out from the mind
Each image unwelcome
That fantasy and jealousy
I am ready to let alone.

In my ear speech
friendly voice

He assured me that you also
Correspond
My passionate love,
Like before,
Perhaps more than before,
What now heavier
The burden of years,
And approaching coveted
The fiftieth year shall turn to
From that before God
And men
We swore to each other
To continue to love us
Till death do Us part.

SINGING AT ION LUCANIA

Shoreline,
then dunes,

plain,
terraces
and hills.
This was the wonderful scenery
That the Greek colonists sighted
After ventured
Along the Ionian coast of Lucania.
They dated with agile boats
The riverine arteries della Lucania
beautiful
Like the fingers of a stiff hand:
Bradano,
Basento,
Cavone,
the Agri
and Sinni.
The first adventurers Achaia
They mingled with the natives.
The second, more experienced farmers,
artisans and merchants,
real colonizers
they settled
in Siris and Metaponto.
They made Magna
The novella Greece:
Siris, Heraclea and Metaponto,
three jewels of the ancient power
Lucan and civilization.
But, alas, by the sweat of his brow
Indigenous, semischiavi
Land, livestock and factories!
Then they sprang jealousy of the Greeks
Taranto, Sybaris and Crotone

And the fratricidal struggle for dominance.
Then came the Romans,
sapped the strength of the Samnites -Lucani.
Ager publicus, estates
And rustic villas,

castrum and cobbled streets.
Everything from Rome,
all the way to Rome,
until the imperial age,
to decline,
the marshes,
Malaria.
Escape to the hills and plains:
Bernalda, Pisticci, Anglona,
Ferrandina Grottole, Tricarico,
Grassano, Timmari, Irsi.
Dioceses, abbeys and convents,
baronies and counties:
autarkic economy
and serfs!
From the Middle Ages to the modern age:
barbarian dominations,
then the Lombards and Byzantines,
Norman and Swabian,
Angevin and Aragonese,
French and Spanish,
Bourbon kingdom of the Two Sicilies.
Still hardship, toil, malaria.
Needless bourgeois revolution of '99,
the fury of Napoleon and the French,
Return of the Bourbons and the Restoration,
Moti Carbonari and Mazzini.
The Garibaldi enterprise,
the annexation to the Kingdom of Savoy,
Italy Units:
Here tick the robbery,
colonization military and economic.
The Southern question,

the dead hand
and the new agrarian bourgeoisie,
even the large estates!
Still semi-slavery
peasants and shepherds!
Until the Reclamation nineteenth-twentieth century,

until the Fascist Integral Reclamation,
until the Agrarian Reform of Postwar.
Massive human intervention
who won the malaria,
He has drained the water,
He ripped pieces of the wood,
he put on intensive agriculture.
But, alas,
the balance man - nature has been broken:
rivers harnessed by dams
and impoverished
do not feed more mouths and beaches.
The sea advances and rode the coast.
A little use artificial dunes
where they are not yet sprung
as if by magic
villages for tourists
and intensive agricultural funds.
SOS for you, or Ionia!
SOS for you, oLucania!
As in symbiosis
They must live
Nature and Culture,
landscape, agriculture and cultural tourism.
It is our task, or Lucania,
to you in particular, shrewd politicians
and our land lovers.

Here laughs the East
And a ray of sunshine
Gilds your clear front
It restores the pink
To your lips soft,

What age do not discolors
Or ripples.
Your eyes shine
As the morning star.
I am filled with the smell feminine
thalamus
And I go into raptures of the perfume
Remarkable that only your
And in no other.

Pout your
More than a day
~~I can not stand.~~
~~Really you do not need~~
~~That your sweet~~

~~Pink lips~~
~~I still ask themselves~~
~~If it is true and only love~~
~~Mine.~~
Since the Fate
~~Everything can ò take off~~
~~Fuorch is the 'my love for you,~~
~~One and only.~~

It never was
And that ever divided
From you my heart.
As it was for famous
Young lovers of antiquity:

Hero and Leander, Pyramus and Thisbe,
Florio and Whiteflower-, Tristan and Isolde,
Lancelot and Guinevere, Paolo and Francesca,
Immortals Romeo and Juliet.
And many others sung by great poets:
Like Dante, who loved Beatrice,
Petrarch loved Laura,
Fiammetta Boccaccio.
And Ariosto and Tasso, who loved
Serenely the first,
Excruciatingly second.
Platonic Leopardi,
Tenderly Manzoni his angelic Henrietta,
Passinonalmente Foscolo,
Manfully Carducci,
The sensually aesthetic D'Annunzio,
Discretamene and melancholy Pascoli,
As well as Ungaretti, Montale, Quasimodo,
Saba, Cardarelli, Luzi.
Do you know why?
Because love is universal
And the poet's heart
It is more tender
For his nature.

The sweet murmur
Of this slow stream.
More sweet are thy words
Who come to the heart
And the heat.
While we too slowly,
Skimming along the path,
In the woods we go

And we admire the multicolored leaves
That gives to the human Fall,
The earth and all those little creatures
There are teeming fans and supplies
For the upcoming harsh winter.
See, fauns and nymphs
They are spying on us and repaired
Behind the Musk trunks,
And await curious and envy
Our kisses
And our impulses.

I placed the head
Soft on your lap
And I aimed the serene stars
Of your pupils,
Glowing in desire of die
In such a sweet and happy state.
You were and are

My hope alive
That you do not ever
Separate from me.
Just I could not tolerate
One of your absence,
Even temporary.
Oh, he could never go out
The fire which for so
You lit in my heart!

The sweet kisses than once
Let me suck
From your lips soft.
painfully remember
The lens caresses
Reddened cheeks
And the ruffled of your hand

On my hair.
Abandonments in my arms
And the faint whispers in their ears.
Your confidence and your outbursts.
Your fears and your uncertainty.
Your innocence of looks and acts.
All this I miss ...
When your face
You darkened.

Here I am again
To ask for forgiveness
For other motivation.
I should have shown
more understanding
Your momentary
Health state

And of the bothering weight
Care of the house and grandchildren,
The latent fear for my fate.
But you see how I burn,
Perhaps hopeless.
See how low port
The lashes, and full of sadness.
How many more times
I'll have to beg?

Which a smelling pink
Dew fresh,
Exit from the shower stall
Wrapped in a bathrobe
Of celestial color.
And here I was eager look
Put a belt round you, in spite of yourself,

In my arms
And I drink one by one
The drops that will fall on your face.
Start your tremor
And our mouths
Frantically
They seek and seal.
this Venus
He intertwined with Adonis
After launderings
At the font when
The handsome young man was returning
Tired and out of breath
The hunts.

How many Sighs
I drew from my chest,
How many tears from my eyes!
That year ominous where
For stupid misunderstandings
And adverse family circumstances
Life gave us away,

You Boiano, I Gravina!
Suffered great wrong
Our love.
Even after so many years
I'm sorry
For my share of the blame.
Sweet, though, comes to mind
Memory
The long-awaited reconciliation.
As you were an early handheld,
While I asked you lose
For the first time
And I confirmed
That my heart was beating
Still strong for you
And were I missed you so much!
What was the consolation
To hear your second "yes."
Yes, I still loved her!

Timeless
It is now
Our love,
Then that lasts
For half a century,
That is, from that first place
My heart leaped in his chest

At the sight of your
Singular beauty:
The Madonna Oval,
Bright, laughing eyes,
Mouth pink and pearly teeth,
Line and perfect roundness,
clear voice
and virginal shyness.
That sight broke my heart!

Time flies
And life is brief dream.
And although it is worth
Live it intensely.
With joys and sorrows, yes,
But it should still live their lives,
Especially if the accompanying

Love.
Which is light, warmth, trust,
Hope, illusion.
Even sorrows and disappointments,
Sure,
But it all makes sense
The earthly journey.
Especially if weak
It is faith in God
And we live in confusion.
Blessed are those who love each
In a voltage to the Creator
Love.

CASTELSARACENO

Here's another wonder
Earth Lucani.
Castelsaraceno, picturesque
"Country of the two parks":

To the west, the wooded Alps Pollino,
to the east the bald mountain Raparo
on the edge of the Parco of the Val d'Agri - Lagonegrese.
Habitats of wolves, eagles and eagle owls, falcons,
otters and blacks peaks.
And kingdom of beech, chestnut and pine trees loricati
Resembling our love armored
Against the voracious time.
Ah, if we were even at a young age!
We would be at the foot of the compact waterfall
Torrente Racanello
And immersed in the pond below
How timid nymph you
And I faun hungry.
We just have climbed the slope
Leading to the forest of chestnuts novellas,
we collect with almost religious rite.
And having witnessed the trunk cut
That thee is like "antenna"
trophy for the bold lucky
that will make firewood for the coming winter
as ancestral custom.
He gave us the couple happiness,
to return by coach,
keeping close your ivory hand
in my loving hands.

Its scents mouth more than pink,
chest ivory smelling,
beautiful face
brighter than the sun of May,

the whole person
harmonious.
And 'This is the great value
my bride.
But even more
The wisdom of his mind
And his advice infallible.

Love,
I do not want to lose you,
and not by instinct male
ownership or insane jealousy,
as sometimes it seems

You want to tell me.
Indeed, I could not help but
of you,
That you are the breath of my soul,
the meaning of my life,
the companion from which ever
I could separate myself,
if not at risk
deep depression
and contempt for life itself.
Love,
still loves me
as I love you,
and more and more.
That not even the afterlife
us part!

No words,
only tender looks
and sighs.
Hand in hand,
along the path
among the thousand colors of autumn.

As teenagers thesis
towards an indefinite happiness,
far from the noise of the world.

A young friend
Skeptical about marriage
And even on the coexistence
Ask me
Such as the most beautiful and compelling moments
Of a couple's life.
And me :

- Sure, if you look around,

the landscape is bleak:
too short parables,
great loves, believed such,
in pieces!
But if there is true love,
made of deep feeling,
before and even more than
physical attraction,
and lasts at least until clearance
painful but fatal partner?
Their increasingly warm hearts,
their busy minds
of sweet memories and nostalgia
of the highlights:
the first dreamy looks,
the first touch, the first kiss,
the first embraces stunning.
And many others like
The embraces to return from work
Or from a trip or adverse events,
The calm after small storms,
the first announcement of maternity-paternity,
the first cries and the first smiles of the infant,
his first steps,
his first pranks.
So, my friend,
not worth it?

The noble poets
The Italian Cinquecento
They sang their man

- - Perhaps unique -

Calling him "my only sunshine."

I hope not delude myself
On this be too
For you.
Merits and certain defects
They had these men,
I am no exception,
Yes I hope you love me
As I am too.
It would still be nice
I want that you idealized me
As I sing
In my prose poems
Of perpetually in love poet
Of your beauty
And your undeniable
Goodness Cross.

So frequent in dreams that disturb me even sleep
deeper, there is no place where I should lose you
and not feel lost me with anguish, thè vain
I follow you and I seek you. Vo licking the fleeting footsteps of your
graceful foot; smelling the scents that scatter your move
and suck the sweet air that she kissed your face.

Vain around his eyes to heaven and earth, to the steps
and alleys in search of your beautiful appearance.
Sometimes I cry - Love, my love, my even if you are, even if you vanish.
Turn back to look intently at him that the heart and the whole life you
have
donated. Oh, if you knew how my poor mind is anxious
in the effort to know where you are and if you're still all mine! -
If it is true that dreams are born deep ego, can not
have a foundation other than the irrational fear to have you
lost forever! Upon awakening, I back the anger and curse
against the doom that I have changed almost latent enemy,
and against you, now towards me so icy. But, he returned to calm,
immediately
I tell myself: - What am I saying, oh that I waver? My love, I'm not, I'm
not
I
that irascible lover!

Divinely tasty
each dish
that devise
Your fairy hands.
Novella Ebe,
At table we learned from Immortals
who experience

The variegated and industrious
Fruits of your art.
precious gifts
Your unconditional love.
Pleasures that color of blue
Our life.
More reason
To love you,
If not enough
Your timeless beauty
And the greatness of your
And your undeniable
Goodness Cross.

If you observe
the backs of my hands,
Spot the watershed
when I arrived at my seventieth:
a lefty almost nothing to variation,
right, the first macules
pre-annoucement of fall or, at least,

of decline.
So in the midst of life expectancy
and dip in a vacuum, of course before you.
Ago ', or divine, that nothing is wasted,
However, of that vibration remains
in real life,
Before it's too late.

Hazel and silver would your hair, if not the painted
brown or dark. But still she keeps me in a snare. nor does it matter
if you melt the wind or in a ponytail twists. Equally
fire me the soul and gives a wound to my heart.
Serena and even beautiful your forehead, where just show up somewhere
nice groove, by way 'of habit, turns on pleasing my chest.

Sickles and arrows are for me your eyelashes. Venus languid your eyes,
still burning, raptors and rebels. Even pinkish your mouth,
witch when he kisses me and suave when it's motto. white
and lascivious your beautiful breasts, even my darling and pleasant garden.
Still have beauty and softness of your slender and warm hands.
promised land, clear sky and sea of beauty you are still for me,
then you will never get old for real!

www.ingramcontent.com/pod-product-compliance
Ingram Content Group UK Ltd.
Pitfield, Milton Keynes, MK11 3LW, UK
UKHW020218250726
13967UKWH00001B/68

9 781326 569044